PERSONAL BOOKLET

JOURNEYS

Copyright © CWR 2009
Published 2009 by CWR, Waverley Abbey House,
Waverley Lane, Farnham, Surrey GU9 8EP, UK.
Registered Charity No. 294387.
Registered Limited Company No. 1990308.
The right of Jeff Lucas to be identified as the author of
this work has been asserted by him in accordance with
the Copyright, Designs and Patents Act 1988, sections
77 and 78.
Questions for group discussion: Jeff Lucas
For a list of our National Distributors visit
www.cwr.org.uk/distributors
Unless otherwise indicated, all Scripture references
are from the Holy Bible: New International
Version (NIV), copyright © 1973, 1978, 1984 by the
International Bible Society.
Concept development, editing, design and production
by CWR.
Printed in the UK by Nuffield Press
ISBN: 978-1-85345-531-5

DAILY READINGS AND GROUP

DISCUSSION QUESTIONS: **JEFF LUCAS**

CWR Applying God's Word
to everyday life and relationships

CONTENTS

INTRODUCTION

THE WORLD IS CHANGED BY DREAMERS.

Martin Luther King Jnr. famously had a dream, articulated it with brilliance and, even though he sensed that he would not live to see the fulfilment of his 'impossible' dream, we now find ourselves living in a world where so much progress has been made in the eradication of racial oppression. The sight of a black man in the White House, once the stuff of far-fetched fiction, is now a reality.

When we look at the challenges of poverty and injustice in the world, they seem overwhelming. But it's not for us to shrug our shoulders and walk away. Micah was a Hebrew prophet who dreamed of something better, and so he sought to prod and nudge God's people into a new place of compassion, care and equity.

So, as we wander through the streets of India and ponder Micah's massive challenge, let's ask the Lord to birth a hopeful dream in us. May we catch His heart and find clear action points to make a difference – as we remember that the world will be changed, one person at a time.

How to use

This resource is
designed to include all
you will need for six
small-group sessions.
It comprises six DVD
clips, icebreakers, group
discussion questions
and prayers based on
each clip and Bible
readings to be used
between each session.

PREPARATION

1. Watch the DVD clip before the meeting.

2. Use the icebreaker to get people chatting. Select the
   questions that you think would be most useful for
   your group to look at. You may want to use them all,
   depending on the time you have available. We suggest
   you plan for 30–45 minutes.

THE SESSION

1. Play the DVD clip first and go straight into the
   icebreaker question.

2. Use the questions you have selected.

3. Move from discussion into prayer. There's a prayer
   included in the material that you could finish with at
   the end.

4. Encourage the group to use the daily readings in
   the days between sessions. The readings expand
   and build on the topics covered in the DVD. If the
   group members are not used to daily Bible reading,
   encourage them to develop this habit. If the group
   members are already into a routine of Bible reading
   and prayer each day you might want to discuss how
   best to work these new readings into their time.

5. You could start the next session by reviewing how the
   group found the daily readings. What did they learn?
   Do they have questions to raise? How did God speak?

Session 1:

Micah, the impossible dreamer?

ICEBREAKER:
Have you ever had a really vivid dream that's stayed with you? Can you talk about it?

FOR GROUP DISCUSSION:
• Does having vision and dreaming get more difficult as we get older? (cf. Joel 2:28)

• 'The kingdom of God comes when a child is released from prostitution or a hungry person is fed.'
  Is this a new idea to you? How does this fit with your concept of the coming of the kingdom of God?

• Read Micah 6:8. How can we live this out?
  What wrong ideas have we swallowed and how can we be open to change?

• What do you understand as the difference between ownership and stewardship? How do you view your 'stuff'?

• Share an example of where you sensed that God gave you a dream … and it came to fruition – or failed. What caused the success or failure?

• How important is it that our radical dreams are tinged with pessimism? Why?

PRAYER:
Lord,
The challenge is immense –
we have so much to learn.
Help me to see Your world
through Your eyes.
Amen.

Resources:
Ronald J. Sider, *Rich Christians in an Age of Hunger* (Word US, 2005)

Shane Claiborne, *The Irresistible Revolution* (Zondervan, 2006)

Marijke Hoek and Justin Thacker, *Micah's Challenge – the Church's Responsibility to the Global Poor* (Paternoster Press, 2008)

THE world was never designed to be a place of poverty, war, terrorism and oppression. In the beginning, God created humanity with a very clear purpose: to know Him. As people made in the image of God, humanity was commissioned to 'take care' of the rest of creation.

Israel in particular was called to be a 'working model', as Isaiah put it, a lighthouse people that demonstrated to the rest of the world what life lived in harmony with God looked like. They were the chosen people, as Christopher Wright says, not selected at the *expense* of the other nations but for the *sake* of them. Enshrined in the laws handed down from God through Moses were principles of compassion and justice (Lev. 19:1–37). One word summarises this radical state of peaceful coexistence that God had in mind: *shalom*, the peace with God that leads to peace within ourselves, with each other, with our environment and between nations. *Shalom* includes wholeness, health, quietness of soul and preservation.

But paradise has been lost. Eight centuries before Christ, Israel had become arrogant and greedy. Times were prosperous for the fortunate well-heeled few – but the poor were being driven off their land, sold into slavery and crushed by heartless land barons who, sickeningly, were religiously pious as well as despotic. Up stepped Micah with a stern wake-up call. A contemporary of Isaiah, Hosea and Amos, he exercised his ministry mainly during the reigns of Ahaz and Hezekiah, and spoke words of thunderous judgment and glorious hope.

As we look around our ravaged world, we remember that God has always called us to live differently.

Prayer: Lord, Your plans for this world were always good. Show me how I can play my part. Amen.

In the beginning

BIG PICTURE:
**Genesis 1:27–28
Isaiah 42:5–8**

FOCUS:
'God blessed them and said to them, "Be fruitful and increase in number; fill the earth and subdue it."'
(Gen. 1:28)

The world was never designed to be a place of poverty, war, terrorism and oppression

Almost everyone can be wrong

BIG PICTURE:
Micah 2:1–11
Amos 7:1–17

FOCUS:
'If a liar and deceiver comes and says, "I will prophesy for you plenty of wine and beer," he would be just the prophet for this people!'
(Micah 2:11)

WE CAN all get it so wrong. As Micah (and we will be staying with him for a little while) grabbed Israel by the throat (figuratively speaking – he does use some very vivid language in his prophecies), we realise that we can drift into a collective slumber about vital issues – and can all be wrong as a result.

The power base of the Temple, perpetuating a cult of worship that was big on ritual and void of compassion, came in for a tongue-lashing from the prophet. And the materialism that was sweeping the land, where large estates were springing up everywhere, with property barons driving the poor from their fields and selling their children as slaves, had to be confronted, especially as the oppressors still took comfort from the vague rituals of their heartless religion.

The political authorities, instead of offering a remedy for the situation, became plunderers themselves, treating the people as if they were sheep for the slaughter (Micah 3:1–4). Judges, priests and prophets did not condemn the injustices but sold themselves to the system, reflecting well the spirit of the society that fed them (Micah 3:9–11). And the rich were disgusted that the prophets would meddle in everyday matters. 'Popular' prophets, who would tell everyone what they wanted for an alcoholic reward, were all the rage. They developed what one writer calls 'a theology of oppression', using Scripture to 'justify' the terrible injustices that were taking place.

Everyone was getting it wrong and deluding themselves into thinking that they were so right. Popular ideas about poverty can be wrong.

We can all get it so wrong

Prayer: Father, help me to see Your truth. Save me from the delusions of myths that are popular – and wrong. Amen.

BEFORE we start to think about what we can do about our poverty-stricken world, we must know that our resources are not really ours – they belong to God. Whatever we have, we don't own – it's all borrowed from the God who provides. We are stewards – those who manage the property of others.

As the relentless rich drove the poor off their land, Micah condemned them, because the land was ultimately part of the blessing of God to His people: not given to them, only lent. They were not owner-occupiers but tenants. The land was to be protected and cared for so that it could be passed on to the care of future generations. Israel had not earned the land but had been given it as a gift as a part of the covenant with Abraham (Gen. 12:1–7; 13:14–18).

Yet a rich class had gradually emerged and come to control the poor. Their riches were made up of huge land holdings, an abundance of cattle, splendid homes and many servants and slaves. In his first concrete prophetic indictment, Micah takes on the landholders and land grabbers, the most active and ruthless among the rich. They had stolen the lives of others – the landless had no option but to surrender themselves to be sold into slavery.

When we think of our 'stuff' as ours, we end up asking the wrong question: 'What shall I give – and how should I use what is mine?' But the truth of stewardship calls us to a different question: 'How would God have me manage what He has entrusted to me for the time being?'

Prayer: Lord, help me live in the truth of stewardship. Save me from grabbing in order to get. Amen.

Nothing is ultimately ours

BIG PICTURE:
Micah 2:1–5
Exodus 19:5–6

FOCUS:
'They covet fields and seize them and houses and take them. They defraud a man of his home, a fellow-man of his inheritance.'
(Micah 2:2)

It's about *people*

BIG PICTURE:
Micah 3:1–12
John 10:1–18

FOCUS:
'You who hate good and love evil; who tear the skin from my people and the flesh from their bones.' (Micah 3:2)

STATISTICS can be overwhelming. When we consider the needs of the world, the figures are mind-boggling and difficult to grasp. India is a good example. Out of around 1.1 billion people, nearly 600 million live in extreme poverty. When women are not valued, millions of them are not taught to read or write and it is estimated that 50 million baby girls have been aborted because they are not wanted. There are 70 million child workers – 500,000 of whom are trapped in prostitution. Two million children live on the streets. The litany of suffering is endless.

But look again. Those figures refer to *people*. They are human beings with hopes and dreams: babies that cry because they're hungry, people who are desperate to escape poverty – but have little hope of doing so.

Micah condemns Israel for treating people like commodities. It was not just that houses and land were stolen – but the lives of *people* were ruined as the oppressors coveted, seized and bullied – all Micah's words. In contrast with God, the Good Shepherd (Micah 2:12), the heartless rich treated the poor like sheep herded into a slaughterhouse. Jesus famously describes Himself as the Good Shepherd who knows His sheep (John 10:14), comforting us with the news that we are far more than a crowd or congregation to Him; each one of us is unique and loved. As we consider the poor, we mustn't lump them together as a faceless underclass but realise that every person has a story and each one matters to God.

Life may be cheap in some oppressive cultures but it's never cheap in the eyes of the God who came to redeem each one.

Prayer: God, give me the gift of empathy, to be able to look past statistics and see hurting people. Amen.

'I'M LIVING the dream' is a statement that sometimes refers to a well-heeled, pampered life. But there's another, greater dream that God has for His earth.

Micah was a dreamer. He looked forward to better days ahead, when the meek would inherit the earth and the land grabbers would be excluded. A double stream would flow in and out of Zion; pilgrim peoples would come and justice and the knowledge of the Lord would flow out (Ezek. 47:1–2; Joel 3:18; Zech. 14:8). Micah was looking for the coming of the kingdom of God. He dreamt of a world where the weapons of war would be discarded in favour of the instruments of peaceful farming. Humanity keeps hoping for the day when military manoeuvres are turned into sports festivals, tanks into tractors and bullets into bread. Then there will be true prosperity and harmony on earth. Walter Brueggemann sees the vine and the fig tree as simple and modest dreams of farmers, not the dreams of kings and generals. I've noticed, when I've met young people trapped in poverty, that they often dream great dreams – not for themselves, but of being able to make a difference in their communities.

Anyone who wants to change the world must be a dreamer. Only those who can imagine what might be, will challenge what is. And yet perhaps our dreaming must be tinged with pessimism. As we seek to see change, we are not surprised when some efforts fail, when corruption thwarts the best initiatives or we have to repeatedly start again. Dreaming pessimists aren't silenced by the hard graft and the sometimes thankless task of world-changing. Micah the dreamer challenges us: are we existing or living the dream – God's dream?

Prayer: Break my heart with the things that break Your heart, O God. Amen.

To dream the impossible dream

BIG PICTURE:
Micah 4:1–13
Acts 2:17–21

FOCUS:
'They will beat their swords into ploughshares and their spears into pruning hooks. Nation will not take up sword against nation, nor will they train for war any more.'
(Micah 4:3)

Anyone who wants to change the world must be a dreamer

SESSION 2:
'He has showed you, O man, what is good …'

ICEBREAKER:
Have you ever witnessed poverty first hand? How did it affect you?

FOR GROUP DISCUSSION:
• Rick Warren confesses that, after years of study, he'd barely noticed all that Scripture has to say about God's heart for the poor. Is that your experience? If you were asked not only for a text about the poor but for a general overview of what the Bible teaches, what would you say?

• Why when it comes to 'measuring' Christian maturity do we tend to value 'spiritual' habits, like prayer and fasting, over practical care for God's world? Should being close to God mean that we pick up God's compassionate heart? Why, in some cases, does that not apparently happen?

• What power do we enjoy? What do you think about this statement: 'Power without love is demonic'?

- Is there a one degree shift you could make in your actions that would directly benefit the poor?

- The priests and 'prophets' of Micah's day were told by the rich not to preach about 'ugly' subjects. Do we feel uncomfortable (or even get upset) when stewardship, giving and money are taught about? If so, why?

PRAYER:

Heavenly Father,
Help me to look again
at my attitudes and actions towards those in need.
Forgive me,
where I have been wrong
or have failed to act as You would wish.
Show me how I can make a difference.
Amen.

Resources:

Dewi Hughes, *God of the poor: a biblical vision of God's present rule* (Authentic Lifestyle, 1997)

Mike Hollow, *A future and a hope* (the story of Tearfund) (Monarch Books, 2008)

Peter Grant, *Poor no more* (Monarch Books, 2008)

Obedience versus emotion

BIG PICTURE:
Micah 5:1–15
John 14:15–21

FOCUS:
'I will take vengeance in
anger and wrath upon
the nations that have
not obeyed me.'
(Micah 5:15)

IT'S right to be moved emotionally when we consider the plight of those who battle against poverty. When Jesus saw the needs of the crowds, He was moved with compassion (Matt. 20:34). But Jesus did more than cry – He sacrificed Himself and suffered because He saw the need. Emotion was turned into action. There's always a danger that, if emotion becomes the indicator of whether we should act or not, we can end up doing nothing if we are not moved.

Our response to the poor is not just based on emotion but rather on obedience. Jesus ultimately went to the cross in obedience to His Father's will (Matt. 26:39). That involved a huge battle – even Jesus struggled with obeying God. What was right mattered more than what He felt.

The message is clear: God *has* shown us; the question is one of obedience. Jim Wallis gives a graphic illustration of just how much Scripture has to say about the poor. A seminary student took a Bible and cut out every reference to the poor with a pair of scissors. 'When the seminarian was finished that old Bible hung in threads. It wouldn't hold together, it fell apart in our hands. This is our Bible – full of holes from all that we have cut out.'*

'Therefore I command you to be open-handed towards your brothers and towards the poor and needy in your land' (Deut. 15:11). God commands us to care and to be open-handed and generous, whatever our mood. Our response to that command is not just an indicator of how much we love our world but of how much we love *Him*.

Prayer: Father, whatever my emotions and feelings, help me to be obedient and so show my love for You. Amen.

*Jim Wallis, *The Soul of Politics* (London: Fount, 1994) p.163.

OUR concern for the poor is rooted in the Person of God, who He is, and also who *we* are, as human beings. As Micah says: 'He has showed you, *O man* ...' (italics mine). Humanity is made in the image of God. We are not animals but image-bearers. G.K. Chesterton said, 'People are equal in the same way pennies are equal. Some are bright, others are dull; some are worn smooth, others are sharp and fresh. But all are equal in value for each penny bears the image of the sovereign, each person bears the image of the King of Kings.' James warns us not to mistreat each other because we are divine image-bearers: 'With the tongue we praise our Lord and Father, and with it we curse men, who have been made in God's likeness' (James 3:9). We cannot logically pretend to bless God and then curse someone who bears His image.

Genesis argues that human life matters because we are made in God's image (Gen. 9:6). Humans are not disposable commodities. Micah uses the phrase that describes God's tender relationship with His own – 'my people' – no fewer than ten times.

Micah's call is obviously to the people of God; some would argue, wrongly, that this means that we should only care for fellow Christians. But God always called Israel to care for the aliens. And while we *are* called to care for our fellow Christians, this is not to be exclusive: 'Therefore, as we have opportunity, let us do good to all people, especially to those who belong to the family of believers' (Gal. 6:10).

Our concern is for all, for all are image-bearers.

Prayer: Lord, rescue me from the amnesia that causes me to forget the value of those marginalised by the world. Amen.

He has showed you, O man ...

BIG PICTURE:
Micah 6:1–16
James 3:9

FOCUS:
'He has showed you, O man ...' (Micah 6:8)

Our concern for the poor is rooted in the Person of God

The heart of it all

FOCUS:
'And what does the LORD require of you? To act justly and to love mercy and to walk humbly with your God.' (Micah 6:8)

WHAT does it mean to 'know' God? The answer to that question is absolutely vital. The Pharisees were convinced that they knew God and His ways well, but completely missed the point of it all. Just as they did, we can fall into the idea that knowing God is about following rules and gathering lots of information about God – and, of course, theology *is* vital. But theology that doesn't lead to action is worthless.

Others, in thinking about knowing God, place great validity on having religious experiences. In some cases, the more bizarre these are, the better. Others see knowing God as the ability to retire into prayerful seclusion and be highly diligent in spiritual disciplines.

But if we reduce everything to just one sound bite, God presents us with a helpful précis through Micah's famous words. Do justly, love mercy and walk humbly with God.

And elsewhere there's another succinct summary as Scripture describes good King Josiah. 'Josiah ... always did right – he gave justice to the poor and was honest. That's what it means to truly know me' (Jer. 22:15–16, CEV). Enthroned at the tender age of eight, he reigned for thirty-one years and initiated some massive reforms when the 'book of the law' was discovered during Temple repairs (2 Kings 22:1–20; 2 Chron. 34:1–33). Josiah's heart of compassion and justice for the poor summed up the essence of knowing God.

Knowing God is not about embracing a vague mysticism that is disjointed from the world and its needs or hungering after yet more epic encounters. Those who truly know Him will know His heartbeat – and that great heart beats for justice and mercy.

Prayer: Lord, I want to truly know You and allow You to change my heart to be more like Yours. Amen.

SPENDING time in India and visiting some of the poorest people on the planet (just today I spent time with a family whose address is listed as 'pavement' – they live on the streets in a makeshift shelter), I was moved not only by their plight but also by their powerlessness. They had absolutely no ability to change their circumstances and are at the mercy of the government, who could on a whim demolish their home and leave them without even a flimsy roof. Their shelter is technically illegal and so they have no recourse in law. They have four children (the mother and her girls sleep inside the tiny shelter, the father and son sleep on the pavement) and the monsoon rains will arrive any day. They are extremely vulnerable. But you and I are in a different position. We have power over our lives and perhaps can take for granted emergency support mechanisms (in the UK) of free health care and unemployment benefits; as well as the luxury of being able to make decisions for ourselves.

A key message of Micah focuses on the use and abuse of power. We have power, which is why God requires something of us: because we can. In Micah's time, the powerful used their might to service their greed. Surely power without love is demonic.

We must not just relieve: we must also empower. The Red Cross has a principle that they will 'consider the poor as dignified human beings, not objects of pity'. Let's act and help others to be able to take action – just because we can.

Prayer: Lord, thank You for the power that I enjoy. Help me to use it to help those without power. Amen.

We've got the power

BIG PICTURE:
Micah 2:1
Micah 7:1–7

FOCUS:
'Woe to those who plan iniquity, to those who plot evil on their beds! At morning's light they carry it out because it is in their power to do it.'
(Micah 2:1)

We must not just relieve: we must also empower

We can change

BIG PICTURE:
Micah 7:1–20
Luke 19:1–10

FOCUS:
'Who is a God like you, who pardons sin and forgives the transgression of the remnant of his inheritance? You do not stay angry for ever but delight to show mercy.'
(Micah 7:18)

AS Micah ends on a note of praise and thanksgiving – primarily for God's greatness as expressed through His forgiving nature – we see that when we are guilty of neglecting or ignoring the poor, we can change, be forgiven and make a fresh start. Perhaps this is vital for us to know.

Some of us might feel that we have lived much of our lives without caring too much about the poor – and so it's too late. But that's not true. There is always today, no matter how limited or uncertain our future. We are not condemned to numbing sameness. Like Zacchaeus, who had used the system to exploit the poor, we too can begin afresh. His stunningly generous restitution – far beyond what would have been expected – reveals that the grabber had become a fabulous giver.

But we will have to face up to guilt. Addressing a conference for a major development charity, a speaker said: 'We don't want to make people feel guilty.' At that point he was interrupted by one of his colleagues, who said, 'Why not? We are!'

But guilt alone can paralyse us and make us feel that we are not good enough to make a difference. Forgiven, we begin again. The older I get, the more I think about the legacy I will leave behind. How about this as a potential epitaph for you and me: 'Surely goodness and mercy followed them all the days of their lives'? A legacy isn't created automatically – it takes time, prioritising and sacrifice to make a lasting impact.

Prayer: Lord, may I start from here, seeing others as You see them. Amen.

The older I get, the more I think about the legacy I will leave behind

SESSION 3:
'He has showed you, O man' … through Jesus

ICEBREAKER:
Have you ever experienced culture shock? Where were you and how did you feel?

FOR GROUP DISCUSSION:
• In what ways did Jesus' teaching advocate an 'upside-down' kingdom? How did His actions match His words?

• How can we show our communities and our world that we really do care?

• Jesus came among us as One 'who served'. How much does your church reflect His attitude of servanthood – within both the community and the wider Church?

• Are women in our society still marginalised? Or is the pendulum swinging the other way? What more can we do to respond to the plight of women worldwide?

• What do you think about doing as Jesus did – and asking the poor and marginalised what they would like us to do for them?

PRAYER:
Lord,
Turn my thinking and my actions around
to reflect Your 'upside-down' kingdom.
Amen.

Resources:
www.compassionuk.org
(for information about Christian child sponsorship)

www.tearfund.org
(working to release millions of people worldwide from poverty)

ALL of this talk of God *showing* us what matters to Him, and the repeated commands and calls of Scripture, could give us an idea of a distant God who simply barks orders but does little more. But that is a totally false picture. The incarnation of Jesus shows that God not only takes the side of the poor; He puts Himself in their place. Jesus took His first breath among the poor. His birth, far more than providing a romantic Christmas card scene, reminds us that His first night on earth was spent in uncomfortable surroundings. And soon after He and His family were fleeing for their lives – becoming refugees in another country.

This is a situation that is repeatedly mirrored in the lives of millions of poor families across the world. In a way that is difficult to fully understand, Jesus is able to look into the eyes of the poor and quite literally affirm: 'I know how you feel.' And while His upbringing was in a working family (in those days, the truly poor were those who had no source of income beyond begging), He did not have a life of ease and riches. Christ came and joined in with the graft of life and the business of survival. He spent much of His time with those who were poor and marginalised.

God has more than just words about the poor. As one translation puts it so eloquently, He has come and pitched His tent among us. Visiting an extremely poor community this week, I realised an uncomfortable truth about myself. I felt privileged to visit – but I didn't want to stay. Investigation is easier than incarnation.

Prayer: Jesus, Your actions speak even louder than words. Show me how to mirror Your heart. Amen.

The show-and-tell God

BIG PICTURE:
John 1:1–14
2 Corinthians 8:8–9

FOCUS:
'The Word became flesh and made his dwelling among us. We have seen ... the glory of the One and Only, who came from the Father, full of grace and truth.' (John 1:14)

God has more than just words about the poor

The kingdom

BIG PICTURE:
Acts 1:1–3
Matthew 6:33

FOCUS:
'After his suffering, he showed himself to these men and gave many convincing proofs that he was alive. He appeared to them over a period of forty days.'
(Acts 1:3)

IMAGINE being enrolled in a special training course led by Jesus; one that lasted for six weeks – after the resurrection. That's exactly what happened for the disciples. Jesus did not immediately ascend to His Father but spent 40 days training and instructing His apostolic team. And the main item on the agenda? The kingdom of God.

That should come as no surprise to us. The kingdom was the main message of Jesus. '"The Kingdom of God" was simply a Jewish way of talking about Israel's God becoming King,' says Tom Wright.* The truth of the kingdom shows us that God is not only interested in the matters of the Church but also in every area of life, including the plight of the poor. It carries the challenge that God wants to reign over all areas of our lives – a vital reminder: 'All too often in Western society, people respond to the message of the evangelist by adding a new compartment to their life,' laments Roy McCloughry.**

It is interesting to see that the leading contender for our kingdom loyalty is money. Jesus specifically selected 'Money' (or 'mammon') as the prime candidate for misguided worship (Matt. 6:24). The living, active Church is called to be the primary sign of the kingdom – a living banquet, a working model of life lived under the love and Lordship of Jesus and a party with an open door policy, where all are invited to come in from the cold and join in.

Prayer: Father, let Your kingdom come and let Your will be done, on earth, as it is in heaven. Amen.

The leading contender for our kingdom loyalty is money

*Tom Wright, *Jesus and the Victory of God* (London: SPCK, 1996) p.203.
**Roy McCloughry, *The Eye of the Needle* (Leicester: IVP, 1990) p.123.

IT'S staggering to think that the wealth of the world's 225 richest people equals the combined annual income of half the world's population. That's a lot of treasure. But, in a culture where riches were considered to be a sign of the blessing and approval of God, Jesus challenged the rich man with the news that his amassing of a personal hoard actually indicated a *lack* in his life. His armfuls of plenty were the symptoms of his selfish preoccupation. While Jesus didn't give exactly the same command to anyone else and so therefore this cannot be used as a template for all, He did call those who followed Him to offload possessions and give to the poor (Luke 12:33).

Surely it all comes down to self. Grilled by an aggressive BBC Radio 4 interviewer recently, a government minister talked of how we should help the developing nations primarily for *our* sake. As we give, he argued, the environment will be spared, our economies will be oiled and the likelihood of international terrorism will be reduced because poverty drives terrorism. In some ways he may be right: there may be spin-offs for self-interest. But selfishness won't change the world. Jesus takes the axe to the root of selfishness and greed and calls us to evaluate our priorities, spending and lifestyle. We need to know what is truly priceless treasure.

We're told that the rich man went away sad, because his wealth was great. His sadness would have continued, because true joy is not found in 'stuff' anyway but in giving and contentment.

Prayer: Save me, Lord, from the alluring glitter of selfish treasure. Amen.

Real treasure

BIG PICTURE:
Matthew 6:19–21
Matthew 19:16–30

FOCUS:
'For where your treasure is, there your heart will be also.' (Matt. 6:21)

Including the excluded

BIG PICTURE:
Luke 10:38–42
Galatians 3:26–29

FOCUS:
'Mary has chosen what
is better, and it will not
be taken away from her.'
(Luke 10:42)

TAMMY Wynette sang that sometimes it's hard to be a woman, in a song that is probably one of the great understatements of music. That's certainly true for many in India, where 170 million women are illiterate because the culture favours males. Gender prejudice has led to a holocaust. Fifty million female babies have been aborted – discarded because they were not the 'right' sex.

In a culture where a pious Jew would happily pray, 'I thank You, Lord, that I was not born a woman', Jesus practised an inclusivity that was radical and disturbing. Women were welcome as His followers and friends. Mary forsook the kitchen (much to the disgust of Martha) and took the shocking posture of an apprentice before her rabbi. She was not rebuked by Jesus – on the contrary, He commended her. And it was a woman, unable to give evidence in a court of law because she was not considered trustworthy, who understood that He was going to die (and so prophetically anointed Him for burial). Women were witnesses of the resurrection (Mary Magdalene was the first to see the risen Christ) and were mocked by the band of cynical male disciples when they declared that Christ was alive. Jesus treated women with respect.

Poverty is not just financial but is also experienced through marginalisation and prejudice. Jesus demonstrated the reality that Paul spoke about, that in Christ, 'There is neither Jew nor Greek, slave nor free, male nor female' (Gal. 3:28). By the way, is it hard to be a woman in your church?

Poverty is not
just financial

Prayer: Thank You that You break down walls of stigma and prejudice, living Christ. Strengthen those who find themselves excluded. Amen.

VISITING the famous centre that Mother Teresa established in Kolkata for the destitute and dying, we chatted with one of the Sisters. She paused during our conversation to adjust the drip feed for a terribly malnourished man who seemed to have little time left. Suddenly I felt a clash of emotions. On the one hand, I despaired that these men and women, abandoned on the street, often filthy and worm-ridden, should have to suffer as they did. And yet, looking into the smiling eyes of the Sister, her apron smeared and dirty, I marvelled at the selfless love that means that these dear ones do not have to die alone. At the very least, their final breaths are taken in an atmosphere of care.

We marvel at the sacrifice of Christ, laying down His life for us at the cross. And yet His action there was not only a work to save but an example to inspire us. So it is that John uses the passion of Christ as an example of how we should care and love. While we may not be called to die for others, we are called to live for them. Love is sacrificial and costly. Paul could write about being 'poured out like a drink offering' (2 Tim. 4:6).

There's one further postscript. That Sister of Mercy was smiling, conversational and happy to ask where we were from. She seemed so full of vibrancy and life even while she tended the dying, although I'm sure that, like Mother Teresa before her, she goes through some very hard times. But living sacrificially brings joy.

Prayer: Father, help me to love when it is costly. May I find the joy that is only discovered in serving. Amen.

Laying down our lives

BIG PICTURE:
1 John 3:16–20
John 15:9–17

FOCUS:
'This is how we know what love is: Jesus Christ laid down his life for us. And we ought to lay down our lives for our brothers.' (1 John 3:16)

SESSION 4:
Excuses, excuses …

ICEBREAKER:

Do you like camping? What would you miss if a tent were your permanent home?

FOR GROUP DISCUSSION:

• We are awash with information and constantly see images of poverty and pain – so how can we avoid 'compassion fatigue'? What's our defence for our lack of action?

• 'We need to partner with others beyond the Church to make a difference.' Do you agree? If you hesitate, why?

• If you knew that Jesus were coming next month, would it make you work harder to serve the poor – or less hard? Why?

• Why do you think that we have moved from participatory to representative democracy?

- What practical steps could you take this week to give hope to someone in need – and begin to change the world one person at a time?

- Do you agree with the development worker who said, 'We *are* guilty'? If so, why? If not, why not?

PRAYER:
Lord,
May I not make excuses
when You are speaking to me
loud and clear.
Use me – not 'them'.
Amen.

Resources:
Ruth Valerio, *Rivers of Justice* (CWR, 2005)

Nicky Scott and Axel Schiffler, *Reduce, Reuse, Recycle* (Green Books, 2004)

Ignorance is not bliss

**Deuteronomy 22:1–4
Luke 10:25–37**

FOCUS:
'If you see your brother's donkey or his ox fallen on the road, do not ignore it. Help him get it to its feet.' (Deut. 22:4)

IT SEEMS like a rather obscure passage of Scripture to consider as we continue our journey, to hear that fallen donkeys are not to be ignored. But, as we think about the needs of a hurting world and find out what God asks us to do to help, we've got to face up to a tendency that is in all of us: to just ignore the problems, put our fingers in our ears, sing a little song and walk away – whatever size the problems are.

Ignorance is bliss, we are told – but it isn't. In fact, ignoring our world has dire consequences. Not only will many continue to suffer needlessly, but our worship will become meaningless and our faith hollow. Moreover, our message of hope to the world will be rightfully ignored if we have much to say about life after death but do little to help others have their basic needs met *before* death. It's too easy to toss the appeal envelope into the bin, to punch the television remote when harrowing scenes appear on our screens and to do nothing other than look the other way. Like the priest and the Levite in the Good Samaritan story, we can pass by on the other side and close our hearts, which then become calloused (Matt. 13:15). But God is the One who 'does not ignore the cry of the afflicted' (Psa. 9:12) and He calls us to be like Him.

Let's consider some of the false ideas that can help us to close our eyes, put our fingers in our ears and cross over to 'the other side'. But let's affirm this: ignorance is not bliss for anyone.

He calls us to

be like Him

Prayer: Lord, open my eyes to painful sights that can change me. Save me from the temptation towards ignorance. Amen.

WHEN we think about trying to change the world, we can quickly feel overwhelmed. We can do so little. Like Jeremiah, we feel inadequate and useless.

The problem *is* huge and there's a lot of bad news. Thousands of children under the age of five die each day from easily preventable diseases and over half the world's children live in poverty. When faced with these facts, it is easy to see why so many people become discouraged. What can I do against an evil dictator or to help a child with malaria? But here is the good news: a third of the world's population claim to be Christian (around 2.1 billion people worldwide). Yes, this covers both the committed and the nominal and, no, we are not suggesting that Christians are the only ones who do good. And we do need to partner with others outside the Church who want to make a difference: we cannot do it alone.

Nevertheless, there are enough of us who call ourselves the followers of Christ to make a serious difference. The tiny Early Church grew rapidly, adding around half a million new members in every generation. By the fourth century there were around five million Christians – about eight per cent of the population of the Roman Empire. Much of this growth has been credited to the fact that the early Christians cared for the poor, touring rubbish dumps and collecting discarded babies – saving them from death or a life of prostitution. The problems were massive; and they, initially, were few. But one by one, step by step, they changed their world forever. We too are salt and light. We too are called.

Prayer: Father, may I hold on to the hope that all actions, both big and small, can change the world. Amen.

I could never do enough

BIG PICTURE:
Jeremiah 1:1–8
Matthew 5:13–14

FOCUS:
'But the LORD said to me, "Do not say, 'I am only a child.' You must go to everyone I send you to and say whatever I command you."'
(Jer. 1:7)

Let God provide

BIG PICTURE:
Matthew 14:15–21
Deuteronomy 15:7–8

FOCUS:
'Jesus replied, "They do not need to go away. You give them something to eat."' (Matt. 14:16)

THE disciples were exhausted and wanted food and a good night's rest. The needs of the hungry crowd seemed beyond them. And so they fell into a common trap: they asked Jesus to do what Jesus wanted *them* to do. He was trying to nudge them into action.

One of the greatest 'spiritual' excuses we can use when we face the issue of a needy world is simply this: 'We'll pray that the Lord will do something.' And we can even be pious about it, something that James, in his no-nonsense epistle, roundly condemns. He marvels at the Christian who uses the traditional Jewish form of farewell as they send the poor away hungry: 'If one of you says to him, "Go, I wish you well; keep warm and well fed," but does nothing about his physical needs, what good is it?' (James 2:16). And lest there are those who think that, because this is written in the context of the Church, we should only provide for fellow Christians, Paul rejects that idea: 'Therefore, as we have opportunity, let us do good *to all people*, especially to those who belong to the family of believers' (Gal. 6:10, italics mine).

There are enough resources in the world to wipe out world hunger. Experts say that there is enough to provide everyone in the world with at least 2,720 kilocalories (kcal) per day. The principal problem is that many people in the world do not have sufficient land to grow their own food or enough money to buy it.

God *has* provided. It's just that what He has given isn't properly shared.

Prayer: Father, I pray that the unjust systems which place gigantic burdens on the poor will be changed. Amen.

God *has* provided

ADAM Curtis, a British documentary maker, recently identified a trend that he dubbed 'Oh Dear-ism.' The premise is that television shows us pictures of terrible things we feel we can't do anything about, including civil wars and starving children. Political conflicts around the world are often portrayed as illustrations of the mindless cruelty of the human race – about which nothing can be done. As viewers, Curtis notes, we feel 'helpless and depressed', and our only response is an 'Oh dear', as if recognising that something is wrong and commenting about it has some merit.

As Christians it's too easy to slip into this mindset. And we can use some nifty ways to make 'Oh dear' sound like it's enough. Humanity is terribly sinful and desperately needs Jesus, we mutter: 'Until the masses turn to God, bad things will continue – Oh dear'.

Some Christians believe that we are in the end times and God's going to end the world soon anyway, so what's the point of making it better? Incredibly, others even resist environmental responsibility on the erroneous notion that, in the big plan, this planet is ultimately disposable. This is false: this earth is going to be renewed and has a place in God's eternal plan.

Slaves used to sing the old spirituals, celebrating a better world to come. But, as they bravely suffered oppression, there were others – many of them Christians – who worked to see those chains broken. Let's not use escapism to evade our responsibilities. Jesus is coming. The early Christians believed that His coming was imminent and worked tirelessly. They didn't see it as a justification for doing nothing.

Prayer: Lord, in the light of Your coming, help me to practically share Your love. Amen.

We're out of here soon anyway

BIG PICTURE:
1 Thessalonians 5:1–28
2 Peter 3:1–18

FOCUS:
'Now we ask you, brothers, to respect those who work hard among you.'
(1 Thess. 5:12)

They should
take care of it

BIG PICTURE:
Isaiah 6:1–8
Ephesians 4:16

FOCUS:
'Then I heard the voice
of the Lord saying,
"Whom shall I send?
And who will go for us?"
And I said, "Here am I.
Send me!"' (Isa. 6:8)

MANY Christians believe in the 'they' people.
Convinced that there are others who need to shoulder
responsibilities that they personally would like to avoid,
they believe that the 'they' people should give to the local
church, work hard to clean the church building, do the
hard work of mission and generally take care of anything
that requires effort. There is a churchwide version of
'they' thinking. When facing up to the needs of the poor,
we can say, 'The Church should take care of that,' as if
the organised body locally has a responsibility to respond
to that with which we don't want to be troubled. Lots of
people who aren't Christians use this little ruse, insisting
that the Church should fix everything that's wrong with
the world, while they themselves are unwilling to open
their own wallets.

And there's a political version too. In a recent article for
the Royal Society of Arts, Paul Ginsborg discusses two
types of democracy – representative and participatory. He
and others have suggested that democracy used to
be focused on *participation* as much as *representation*
(volunteering as much as voting). However, in our
modern society, the democratic process has become
far more passive and is now dominated by the idea of
representation, whereby an elected representative (a local
councillor, MP etc) is held responsible for meeting the
needs of those who voted (or who didn't vote) for them.

It's not someone else's job to change the world. As
Isaiah saw as he volunteered his life to God, it's a task for
all of us. Paul talks about each part of the body doing its
work. What's *our* work?

What's *our* work?

**Prayer: Lord, help me to see what You are calling me
to. Amen.**

SESSION 5:
Here comes the judge

ICEBREAKER:
Have you ever lost your voice? How did you feel when you couldn't make yourself heard?

FOR GROUP DISCUSSION:
- 'God is biased towards the poor.' Do you agree? If that's true, how should it affect what we do and the way we live?

- How can we constructively evaluate the way we live? Can we help one another in the process?

- Discuss some of the advocacy and campaigning organisations you might support and sign up to that will enable your voice to be heard.

- If seeking 'social righteousness' is supposed to be our priority, what does that say about the activities and programmes of our churches?

- Why do you think that many of our youth have such a sense of social concern and a passion for justice?

- Visitors from overseas have commented on the high level of social engagement and concern for the world's poor they see evidenced in the British Church. Is that true of your church? Have attitudes in the Church towards social engagement changed over the last few decades?

PRAYER:
Lord,
Give me the courage
to speak up against injustice –
and the wisdom
to know what I can do.
Amen.

Resources:

Steve Chalke, *Stop the traffik* (Lion Hudson plc, 2009)

Dave Westlake and Esther Stansfield, *Lift the label* (Authentic Lifestyle, 2005)

Leo Hickman, *A life stripped bare* (Eden Project Books, 2006)

MOST of us associate justice with punishment for a crime. It is not a word that we warm to. As one who automatically flinches and feels guilty whenever a police car appears behind my car (even when my driving is perfect), justice is an intimidating word. But the Bible shows that God's idea of justice is not just about punishing people when they do wrong, but rather about protecting people from the wrong done by others.

God is just and He calls for justice. In the Old Testament, He is described as 'the Rock' (Deut. 32:4) – a symbol of stability and consistency. When God called His people to holiness, it included caring for the poor, the elderly, the aliens and those with disabilities (Lev. 19:2–34). It also required honest business dealings – a reflection of God's own rock-like character.

Sadly, righteous men, such as Job, were rare in Israel. God's righteousness was too often a contrast to that of His people – especially those in power. In Indian, Chinese, African and South American civilisations, the power of the gods was channelled through the power of certain powerful males – the priests, kings and warriors embodied divine power. But in Israel's rival vision, it is the 'orphan, the widow and the stranger' with whom Yahweh takes His stand.

So with His 'bias' to the poor, is God being unjust? Vinoth Ramachandra says: 'In a sinful world where life is biased towards the wealthy and the powerful, God's actions will always be perceived as a counter bias.'*

God loves justice

BIG PICTURE:
**Amos 5
James 1:27**

FOCUS:
'But let justice roll on like a river, righteousness like a never-failing stream!'
(Amos 5:24)

Prayer: Lord, the poor need justice, not charity. Be their rock, their deliverer, and show me how to live justly. Amen.

*Howard Peskett & Vinoth Ramachandra, *The Message of Mission* (Leicester: IVP, 2003) p.112.

God is just

SESSION 5: DAY 2

Considering our lifestyle

BIG PICTURE:
Isaiah 3:14–24
Isaiah 10:1–2

FOCUS:
"'What do you mean by crushing my people and grinding the faces of the poor?' declares the Lord, the LORD Almighty.'
(Isa. 3:15)

… we can make

changes that

are a matter of

life and death

for others

IN A consumer culture, we must ask tough questions about how we live. Are there radical – and small – changes that we can make? Every one of us may well respond differently but, however we work out these difficult issues, we must surely respond. Sometimes, in trying to answer questions about our lifestyle, we can resort to unhelpful legalism, accepting someone else's life choices or teaching unthinkingly. And then, excusing ourselves that we don't want to be legalistic, we do nothing. But daily choices change others' lives.

Melba Maggay was involved in the quiet revolution that transformed the Philippines. She speaks eloquently about the difference each one of us can make: 'So this we believe: a kingdom of justice and righteousness has begun and it is making its way into people's lives and denting structures that continue to oppress and dehumanise. Such work is seldom done in the corridors of power nor in the halls of the great. Often it is in the many small acts of integrity and goodness that many faceless men and women do every day, believing that behind the face of an evil that is strong is an unseen good that is stronger, even when it wears the face of weakness. It is this daily practice of hope which keeps most of us going, keeping the monsters at bay as humbly and powerfully we are caught up in the kingdom fire and the stubborn grace that shines at the heart of existence.'*

As we consider our lives, we can make changes that are a matter of life and death for others.

Prayer: Father, show me how to live in a way that pleases You. Grant me wisdom, in Jesus' name. Amen.

*Melba Maggay, *Transforming society* (Institute for Studies in Asian Church and Culture, 1996) p.100.

JUST feeding the poor will not change a world whose economic systems are geared to over half of the world's children living in poverty. When an entire system is inherently unfair, you have systemic sin; not just individuals and their choices, but the way the system is set up is wrong. Micah was confronting not only rotten people but a rotten system of corruption that affected all the judges, priests and prophets.

Many will know of the debt crisis already through the excellent work of (what was) Jubilee 2000. This is the situation in which banks, rich with money from oil in the seventies, lent huge sums of money to poorer countries, with low interest. An economic crisis, however, meant that interest rates increased at the same time as the price fell for basic commodities (the sorts of things the poorer countries were producing: coffee, sugar etc). Countries thus found themselves paying increasing amounts for their debts, whilst receiving less and less from their exports. The result was that the rich countries got more and more money from the poorer countries, which then grew increasingly impoverished. And so we reached the situation where, by 2000, for every £1 given in aid, £13 came back in debt repayments and the basic needs of health care and education were sidelined. The poor became poorer because of the system. And the present credit crunch is making it worse.

Advocacy is a vital part of walking with the poor, because we use our voices to defend those who have no voice: the system has silenced them. Let's use our voices to call for change.

Prayer: Father, show me the best way to add my voice to call out on behalf of the voiceless. Amen.

Speak up against unjust systems

BIG PICTURE:
Proverbs 31:8–9
Micah 3:11–12

FOCUS:
'Speak up for those who cannot speak for themselves, for the rights of all who are destitute.'
(Prov. 31:8)

Prioritise true righteousness

BIG PICTURE:
Proverbs 29:7
Isaiah 58:1–14

FOCUS:
'The righteous care about justice for the poor but the wicked have no such concern.'
(Prov. 29:7)

WE MOSTLY know of the idea of righteousness through the New Testament where the emphasis is on 'being made right before God' through Jesus. Whilst this emphasis should not be lost, in the Old Testament the idea of righteousness is often accompanied by the idea of justice (1 Kings 10:9; Job 37:23; Psa. 33:5; Hosea 2:19). The root word for righteousness, *tsdq*, is used to describe straight paths (Psa. 23:3) and correct weights (Lev. 19:36; Deut. 25:15).

When we come to the New Testament, the Hebrew word for justice rarely occurs, whereas the word for righteousness occurs often. Because of their inseparably close connection, many New Testament scholars think that the word 'righteousness' in the New Testament (*dikaiosune*) should be translated as 'righteousness and justice'. This gives a new force to verses such as Matthew 6:33, where we are told to 'seek first his kingdom and his righteousness'.

Pete Phillips says: 'righteousness ... has something to do with personal piety but *everything* to do with living a life which is in accord with the standard of justice set by God. This standard does not just involve the way we live our personal lives. It involves the way we react with the society in which we live. Isaiah 58 makes it clear that our lives should be based on justice – upon values which bring liberation for the oppressed and release the chains of injustice.'*

This is true righteousness – and God calls us, as kingdom people, to pursue it as our major priority.

Prayer: Lord, show me *how* to seek first Your kingdom and Your righteousness. Amen.

*Pete Phillips: quoted in Jeff Lucas, *The King of the Hill* (Uckfield: Spring Harvest Publishing, 2001) p.45.

THE doctrine of impassivity teaches that God is never moved emotionally – and I think it is wrong. God is moved by the oppression of the poor; He *loves* justice and He *hates* pious but irrelevant spirituality. Through Isaiah, He pleads with His people.

God is just because He loves. His justice is rooted in His faithfulness, His solid, steadfast loving-kindness. We need to listen to the youth culture, where there seems to be such a passion for world justice issues. If we fail to do so, the Church will become, to quote Bishop Pete Broadbent, 'irrelevant'.

In 1986 Yoweri Museveni became President of Uganda, when his National Resistance Army overthrew the military junta. Museveni had attended Christian youth camps during his teenage years and, while at one of the camps, had asked that an evening be devoted to prayer for nearby Tanzania which, at the time, was engaged in terrible civil war. He was told that this request was inappropriate: 'We don't concern ourselves with things like that.' Prayers were held but they focused on the needs of the camp and the spiritual wellbeing of those attending the event. Museveni made a decision: Christianity apparently had nothing to say about the needs of the day, so he would look elsewhere for a guiding philosophy for real life. But he was rejecting a message that was actually a tragic misrepresentation: holiness has justice at its very heart.

Let's ask God to fill us with His passion to serve the poor and, as we do so, perhaps a younger generation will want to come and join us in the fight.

Prayer: Lord, give me Your passionate heart. Help me to listen to the heart of those who love justice and mercy. Amen.

Loving mercy: embrace God's passion

BIG PICTURE:
Hosea 11:8
Isaiah 55:1–3

FOCUS:
'How can I give you up, Ephraim? How can I hand you over, Israel? … My heart is changed within me; all my compassion is aroused.'
(Hosea 11:8)

God is just because He loves

SESSION 6:
Walk humbly with your God ...

ICEBREAKER:
What is your favourite childhood memory? Share it with the group.

FOR GROUP DISCUSSION:
• Some Christian relief programmes insist that those being fed listen to a gospel presentation. In the light of the challenge of personal as well as circumstantial transformation, is this a good idea?

• Why, when we work with the poor, do we face the temptation to stop acting like servants and end up inflicting our own 'good ideas'? How can we prevent much time and money being wasted on 'solutions' that don't solve anything?

• The call for environmental responsibility has increased over the last decade. What changes have you made? What changes are needed? How can Christians model concern for the environment?

- How could we more effectively encourage each other to engage in serving the poor?

- Watch the short extract about the work of Compassion at the end of the DVD. Consider becoming a Compassion sponsor.

PRAYER:
Lord,
You are the God
of the impossible.
May my actions,
through Your power,
help to bring change and hope
to impossible situations.
Give me Your dreams.
Amen.

Resources:

Ruth Valerio, *Life Issues – Environment* (CWR, 2008)

Ed Walker, *Reflections from a scorched earth* (Monarch Books, 2007)

Ruth Valerio, *L is for lifestyle* (IVP, 2004)

Dave Bookless, *Planetwise* (IVP, 2008)

James Jones, *Jesus and the Earth* (SPCK, 2003)

Poverty is not just spiritual

BIG PICTURE:
Matthew 4:4
Philippians 2:14–16

FOCUS:
'Jesus answered, "It is written: 'Man does not live on bread alone, but on every word that comes from the mouth of God.'"' (Matt. 4:4)

PEOPLE need more than food – or, to put it another way, man cannot live by bread alone. I am not suggesting that we should only be involved in aid that includes sharing the gospel, and the Church needs the help of those agencies that do not do so – but we must remember that poverty is not just about money and things. People need the transforming hope that only Christ brings. We are those who 'hold out the word of life' to a world that is hungry for Jesus – whether they know it or not. He is the true bread.

The Bishop of Liverpool, James Jones, says, 'The regeneration of our communities is an absolute priority … and that regeneration has got to be not just economic. It's got to be spiritual and moral, too.' Some politicians agree. Member of Parliament and Christian leader Gary Streeter says, 'There is a growing recognition that the state can do many things well but it cannot deliver the personal or spiritual support that we all need to overcome life's greatest adversities.' Community regeneration is impossible without personal regeneration. Social reform will never come about exclusively through externals, through government, the voluntary sector or church community improvement programmes. There can be no significant, in-depth social transformation without inner spiritual transformation.

The transformation of society is dependent ultimately on the transformation of individuals. People have to change, one by one. The deepest poverty isn't a material problem, it is a spiritual problem. Personal, internal change is an essential ingredient in real social transformation. Therefore, sustainable external change is always dependent on internal change. Let's pray and work for both.

People need

more than food

Prayer: Lord, change my heart and change the hearts as well as the circumstances, of the poor. Amen.

IT WAS one of the saddest sights of my life. To see the devastated coastline of Banda Aceh, Indonesia, flattened after the Boxing Day tsunami, was awful beyond words. And then we put a face on the tragedy as we met Didi and Rosa who run a little coffee shop and petrol station, serving coffee at five cents a cup. They had lost all four of their children, together with their own parents and siblings, as the monster wave swept into the town.

And yet there was another sad sight to come. I looked at rows and rows of houses that had been built by a well-known charity but were completely deserted, because there were no shops or schools nearby. They were completely useless. Apparently the charity had dashed in with a mandate from a donor to build homes. In another community a school had been built – but this locality was also deserted, because what was really needed was simply water.

Jesus asked a question of the blind man that might seem superfluous; but He wanted to listen. Friends of mine with disabilities, who use wheelchairs, tell me of their frustration when they respond in Christian gatherings for prayer. Often people assume they want healing and freedom from the chair; they may have marriage problems, financial challenges – or a headache.

Our task is not to provide what we think the poor need. Our role is to listen, serve and partner with those who have experience. We do not just respond to fulfil an emotional need in us; rather we adopt the posture of servants who will walk with the poor and not just corral them with our 'helpful' solutions.

Prayer: Lord, may I listen first, and then listen again. Amen.

Listen, ask, partner

BIG PICTURE:
**Matthew 20:20–28
Mark 10:46–52**

FOCUS:
'Whoever wants to become great among you must be your servant ... just as the Son of Man did not come to be served, but to serve.'
(Matt. 20:26–28)

Be environmentally responsible

BIG PICTURE:
**Psalm 146:1–10
Leviticus 25:1–24**

FOCUS:
'... the LORD his God, the Maker of heaven and earth, the sea, and everything in them – the LORD, who remains faithful forever.'
(Psa. 146:5–6)

THE richest 20 per cent of the world (ie us!) use 80 per cent of the world's resources. The call for justice demands that we care for God's creation, because climate change is a key justice issue. Psalm 24 gives the name of the legal owner of the earth: 'The earth is the LORD's, and everything in it' (Psa. 24:1). We are only tenants, but our misuse of what God has lent us means that the planet is rapidly heating up. The world's poorest communities are feeling the greatest impact of climate change. As floods, droughts and storms increase, climate change threatens to create millions more 'environmental refugees'. According to the World Health Organisation, 150,000 people are already dying annually as a direct result of climate change. It is predicted that 182 million people will die in Africa alone by the end of the century, unless urgent action is taken by governments and citizens worldwide.

The facts seem plain. 'The scientific debate about whether climate change is really happening is over – it is happening fast and the evidence is overwhelming,' says Andy Atkins of Tearfund.

And we are part of the solution: 'Climate change involves all of us as we share the same atmospheric resources. The question is: are we ready to give our lifestyles a critical look and see if we are causing damage to our neighbours and indeed the generation that is to come after us?' asks Tadesse Dadi, a Tearfund worker in Ethiopia.

Once again, let's realise that small choices made daily can change – and even save – the world.

Prayer: Lord, the earth is Yours. Help me to live each day with responsibility and stewardship. Amen.

TWO men have been very visible when it comes to calling the world's leaders and those of us in what is known as the 'First World' to take radical action for justice for the poor: Bono, of U2, and Sir Bob Geldof. Both Live Aid and later Make Poverty History have been incredibly influential in raising awareness and nudging the leaders of nations to take action to see debt cancelled and trades practices made more just. There's a long way to go, but a great start has been made. Sir Bob rightly said, 'Africa is dying, not of poverty but of politics.' We need people like him to ask the tough questions; Dom Helder Camara, a former Brazilian bishop, said, 'When I give food to the poor, they call me a saint. When I ask why the poor have no food, they call me a communist.'

But, as we get involved in these issues, it is easy to become self-righteous and to start judging those who haven't started thinking them through yet. As we seek to encourage others to consider their lifestyles, buying choices, approaches to the environment, support of advocacy campaigns, giving and a host of other issues, surely a nudge is better than a rant. We must speak up but let's do so in a way that invites people rather than just makes them feel guilty and miserable. We have to extend grace in all our dealings with others – even when the issues seem so crystal clear to us that we cannot understand why they are not to everyone.

In encouraging others to serve a stricken world, kind conversation will surely be more effective than bullying.

Prayer: Lord, help me both with the way I share the message of the world's needs and the tone. Amen.

Encourage others

BIG PICTURE:
1 Timothy 5:1
1 Thessalonians 5:1–11

FOCUS:
'Do not rebuke an older man harshly, but exhort him as if he were your father.' (1 Tim. 5:1)

... it is easy to become self-righteous

Get involved with a bigger organisation

BIG PICTURE:
Philippians 1:3–6
2 Corinthians 8:23

FOCUS:
'In all my prayers for all of you, I always pray with joy because of your partnership in the gospel from the first day until now.' (Phil. 1:4–5)

WE CHRISTIANS are good at reinventing the wheel. Often local churches, without the real knowledge or expertise to ensure proper monitoring, spend large sums of money setting up schemes to help others. Frequently there are other organisations who are experts in the same field.

Compassion is one such organisation. I have observed a 'ripple' effect in their ministry. A child is obviously helped, for there is a safe place where they will feel loved, will hear the good news about Jesus and be provided with nutritious food, clothing and health care. There are opportunities for skills development and a university education that can break the cycle of poverty. But that's just the beginning. Social workers visit the child's home and share helpful information about hygiene and health care with the parents. That information is then filtered out into the community; suddenly everyone knows that washing in the same water that your cattle use – and worse still, drinking from it – is not a good idea.

And then the church is impacted. No one needs to go to a Compassion partner church to teach about how vital social action is: they are living that truth every day. The body of Christ is strengthened and the wider community sees a church that is preaching and doing, truly a sign and wonder. And those of us who partner benefit, as our children see that there is a hurting world beyond their own horizon of mobile phones, gadgets and 'the good life'.

We can change our world. But just as Paul worked with others for the sake of the gospel, we don't have to go it alone.

We can change
our world

Prayer: Lord, show me how I can partner with others, so that I might fulfil Your command to live beautifully. Amen.

Other titles in the Life Journeys series

Singing in the Rain
Navigate life's rough waters with confidence
and poise. Six-week resource – **ideal for Lent**.
EAN: 5027957001183

Life Journeys – Lost and Found
Discover how we can create caring church
communities that make people want to stay
and that encourage prodigals to come home.
EAN: 5027957001237

Elijah – Prophet at a Loss
Take courage from the challenges Elijah faced
in his walk with God.
EAN: 5027957001107

Only £18.99 each
(DVD pack includes a personal booklet)
Extra personal booklets available: **£2.50 each**
(except Singing in the Rain at £3.50)

Other titles also available. For full listing and for more details,
including video excerpts, visit www.cwr.org.uk/journeys

Prices correct at time of printing

Trusted all Over the World

CWR HAS GAINED A WORLDWIDE reputation as a centre of excellence for Bible-based training and resources. From our headquarters at Waverley Abbey House, Farnham, England, we have been serving God's people for over 40 years with a vision to help apply God's Word to everyday life and relationships. The daily devotional *Every Day with Jesus* is read by nearly a million readers an issue in more than 150 countries, and our unique courses in biblical studies and pastoral care are respected all over the world. Waverley Abbey House provides a conference centre in a tranquil setting.

For free brochures on our seminars and courses, conference facilities, or a catalogue of CWR resources, please contact us at the following address.
CWR, Waverley Abbey House, Waverley Lane, Farnham, Surrey GU9 8EP, UK

Telephone: +44 (0)1252 784719
Email: mail@cwr.org.uk
Website: www.cwr.org.uk

CWR Applying God's Word
to everyday life and relationships